DATE DUE

FEB 0 3 2012	

SandCastle™

Baby
African Animals

It's a Baby
Baboon!

Kelly Doudna

Consulting Editor, Diane Craig, M.A./Reading Specialist

ABDO
Publishing Company

Published by ABDO Publishing Company, 8000 West 78th Street, Edina, Minnesota 55439.

Editor: Liz Salzmann
Content Developer: Nancy Tuminelly
Cover and Interior Design and Production: Mighty Media
Photo Credits: Brand X Pictures, Digital Vision, Creatas, Peter Arnold Inc. (Jean-Paul Chatagnon, M. & C. Denis-Huot, Jean-Michel Labat), ShutterStock

Library of Congress Cataloging-in-Publication Data

Doudna, Kelly, 1963-
 It's a baby baboon! / Kelly Doudna.
   p. cm. -- (Baby African animals)
 ISBN 978-1-60453-150-3
 1. Baboons--Infancy--Juvenile literature. I. Title.

QL737.P93D68 2009
599.8'65139--dc22
                         2008005467

SandCastle™ Level: Fluent

SandCastle™ books are created by a team of professional educators, reading specialists, and content developers around five essential components—phonemic awareness, phonics, vocabulary, text comprehension, and fluency—to assist young readers as they develop reading skills and strategies and increase their general knowledge. All books are written, reviewed, and leveled for guided reading, early reading intervention, and Accelerated Reader® programs for use in shared, guided, and independent reading and writing activities to support a balanced approach to literacy instruction. The SandCastle™ series has four levels that correspond to early literacy development. The levels are provided to help teachers and parents select appropriate books for young readers.

Emerging Readers
(no flags)

Beginning Readers
(1 flag)

Transitional Readers
(2 flags)

Fluent Readers
(3 flags)

SandCastle™ would like to hear from you. Please send us your comments and suggestions.
sandcastle@abdopublishing.com

Vital Statistics

for the Baboon

BABY NAME
there is no special name

NUMBER IN LITTER
1

WEIGHT AT BIRTH
1 to 2 pounds

AGE OF INDEPENDENCE
5 years

ADULT WEIGHT
30 to 90 pounds

LIFE EXPECTANCY
30 years

Baboons live in family groups called troops.

Troops usually have about 50 members.

A baby baboon rides on its mother's back.

Mother baboons carry their babies for the first month.

Baboons are omnivores. Their diet is mainly vegetarian but they will eat meat if it is available.

Adult baboons are careful to not hurt the babies. Sometimes a male baboon will hold a baby to keep other baboons from fighting with him.

Baboons use grooming as a way to bond with each other.

Baboons have many ways of communicating. They grunt, bark, and scream. They also yawn and smack their lips.

Baboons live in a variety of habitats. But wherever they are, they sleep above the ground to stay safe from predators.

Leopards prey on baboons. Male baboons show their teeth and scream to try to frighten leopards away.

Male baboons leave their birth troop when they are five years old. Females stay in the same troop.

Young females have the same status within the troop as their mothers.

Fun Fact

About the Baboon

A baboon's canine teeth can grow as long as two inches.

2 inches

1 inch

0

Glossary

canine tooth – one of four front pointed teeth of a mammal.

communicate – to share ideas, information, or feelings.

expectancy – an expected or likely amount.

groom – to clean the fur of an animal.

independence – no longer needing others to care for or support you.

omnivore – one who eats both meat and plants.

predator – an animal that hunts others.

prey – to hunt or catch an animal for food.

status – the position of an individual compared to others in a society.

troop – a group of people, animals, or things.

vegetarian – made up of only vegetables.

To see a complete list of SandCastle™ books and other nonfiction titles from ABDO Publishing Company, visit **www.abdopublishing.com**.

8000 West 78th Street, Edina, MN 55439

800-800-1312 • 952-831-1632 fax